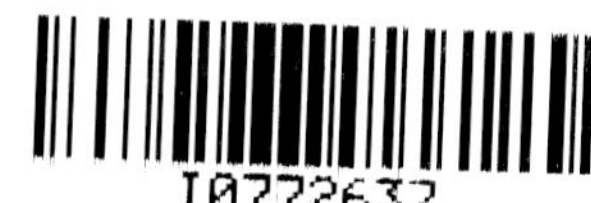

DATE : ....

NAME : ....

AGE : ....

CITY : ....

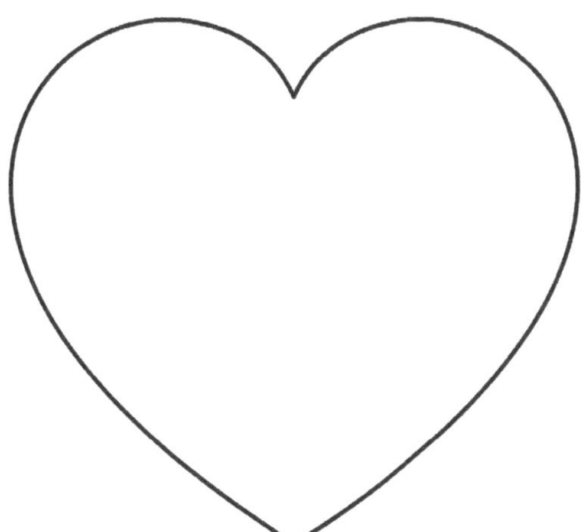

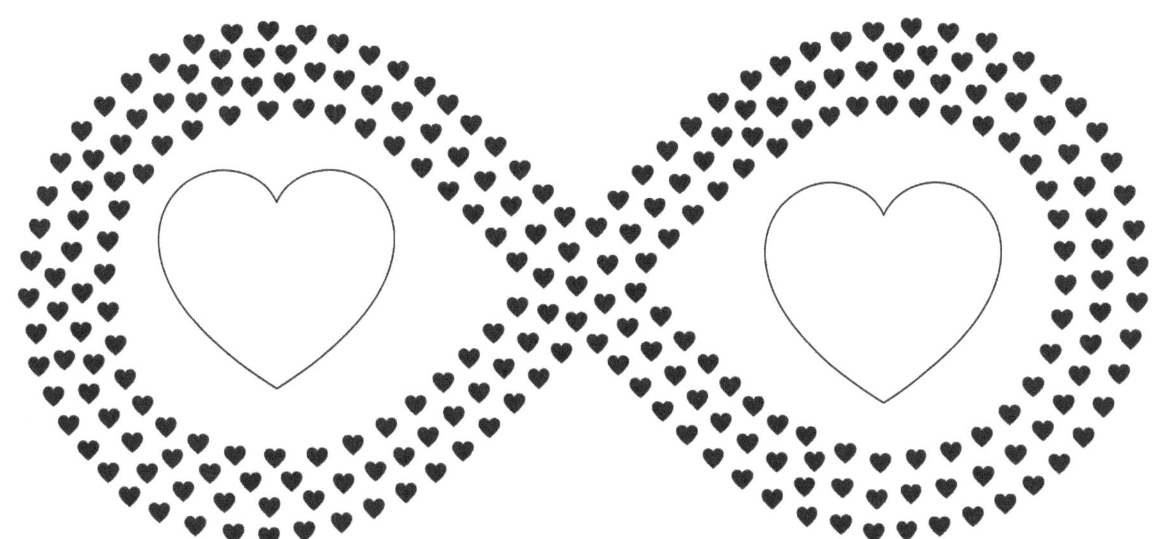

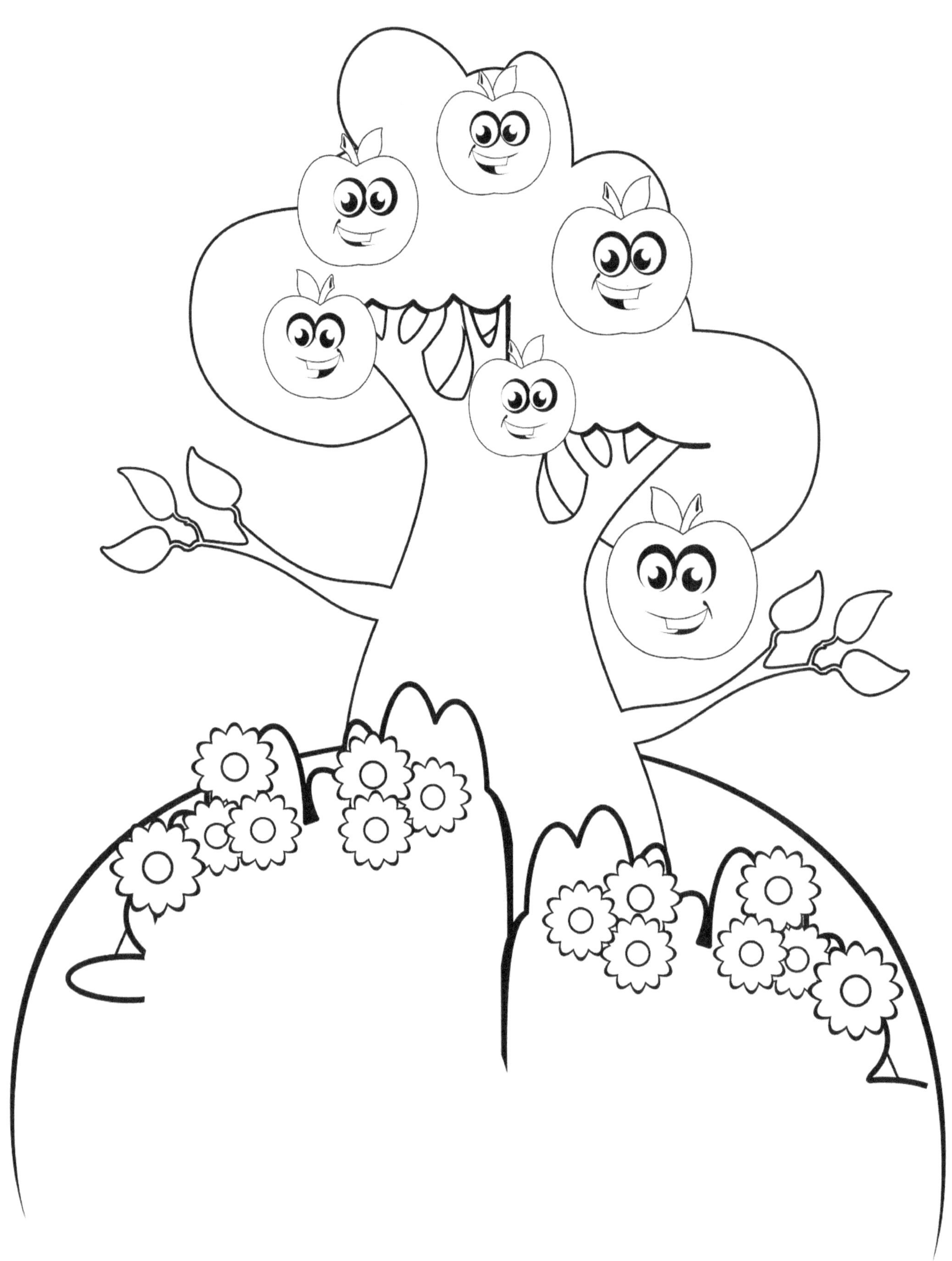

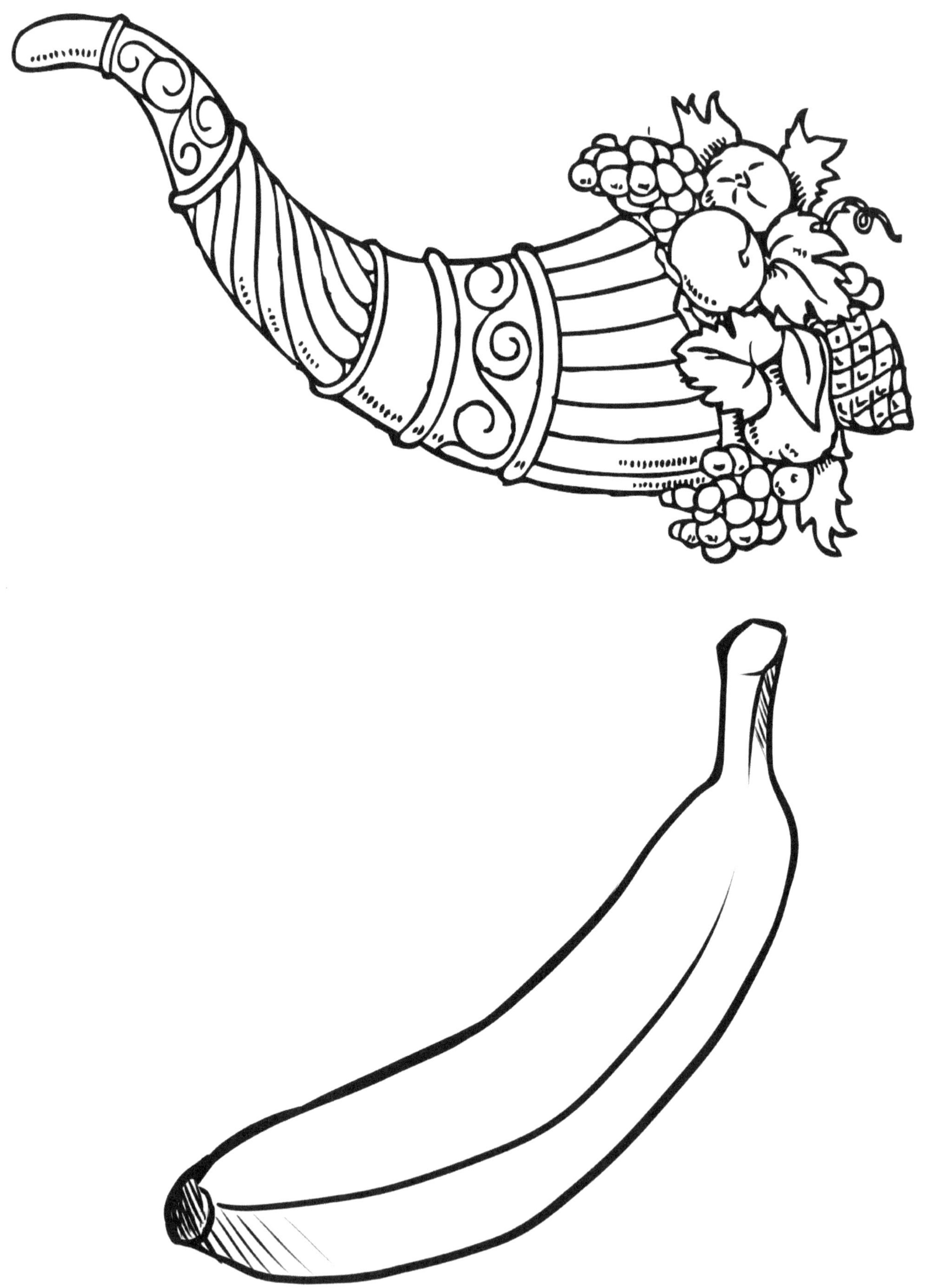

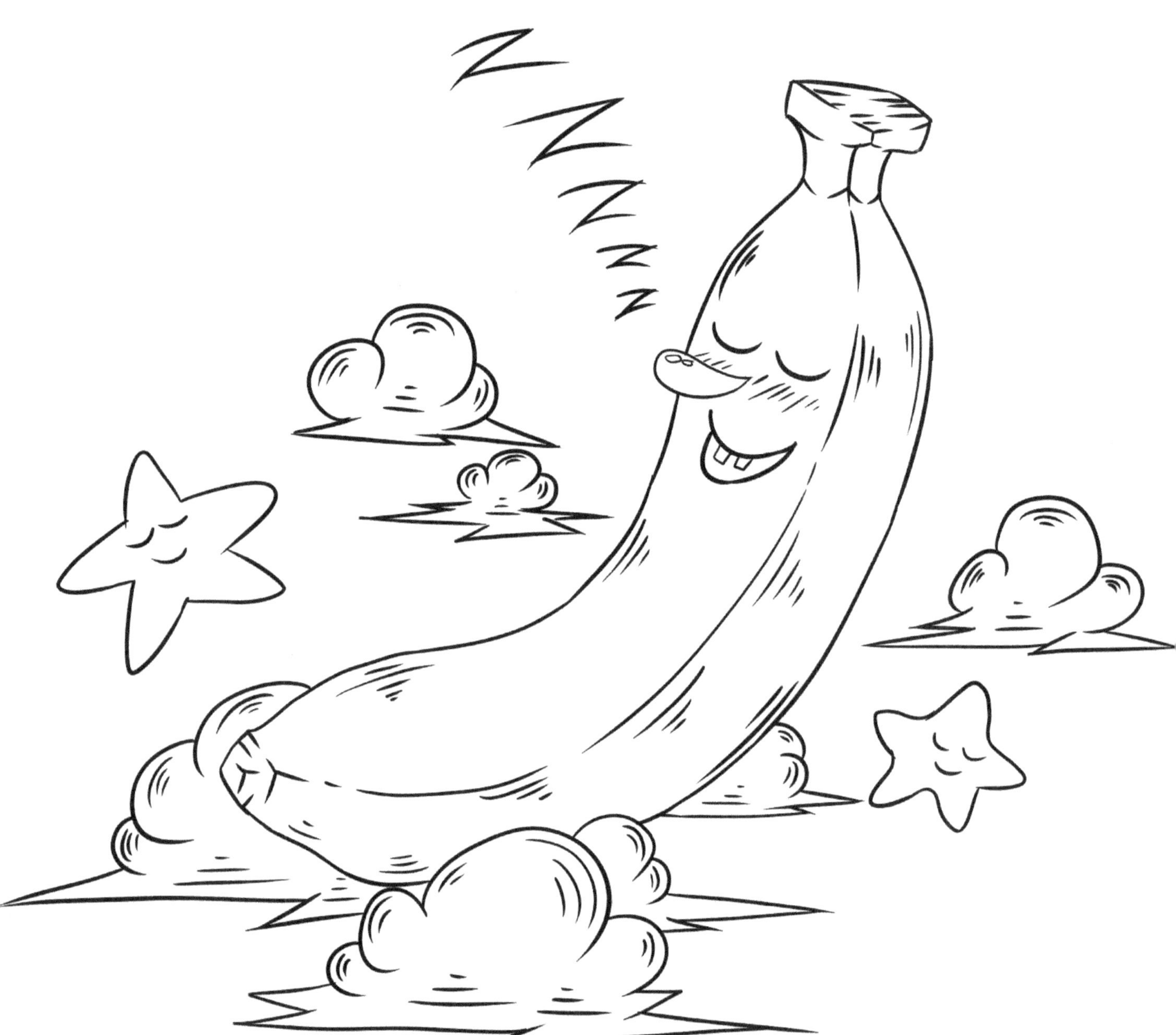

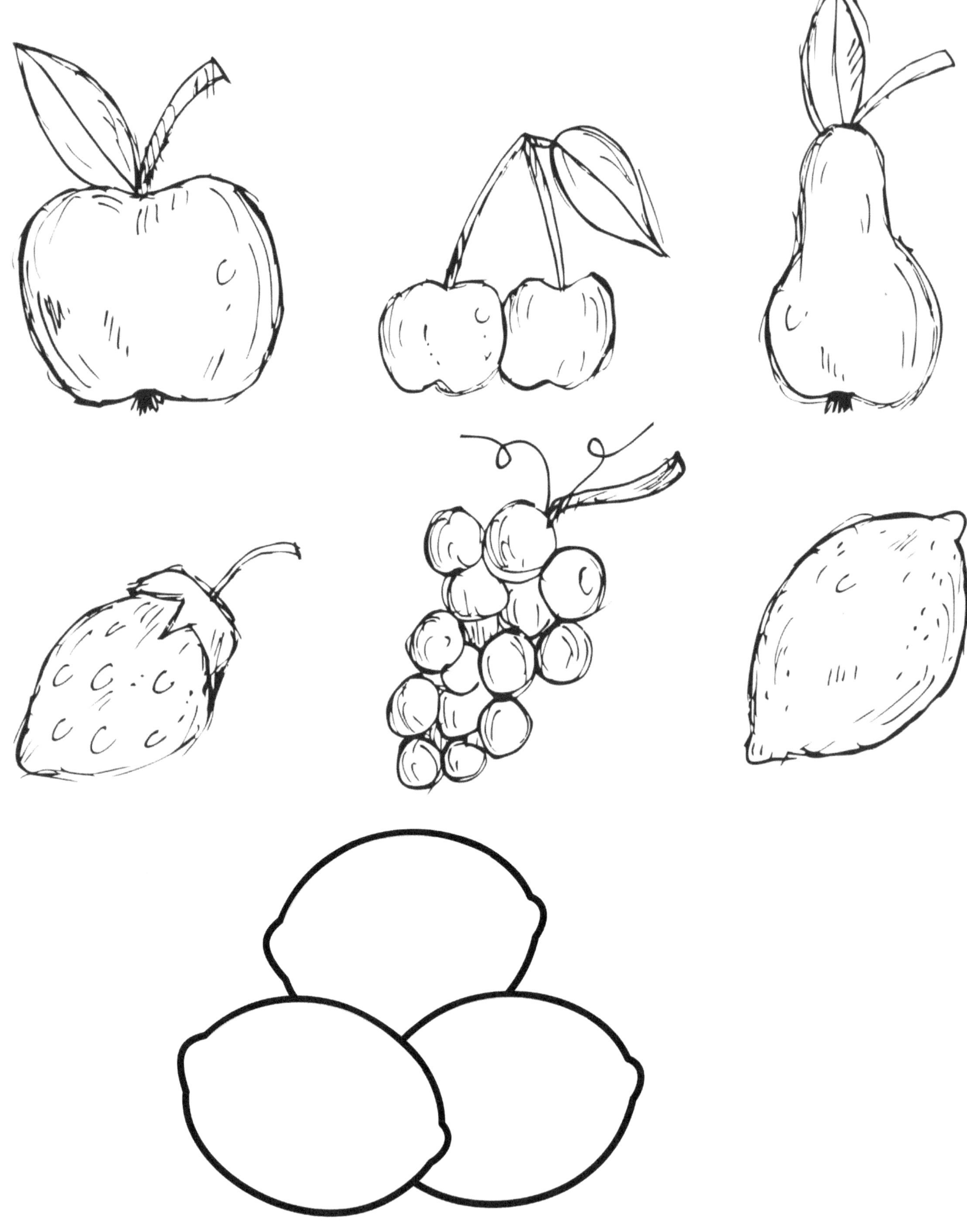

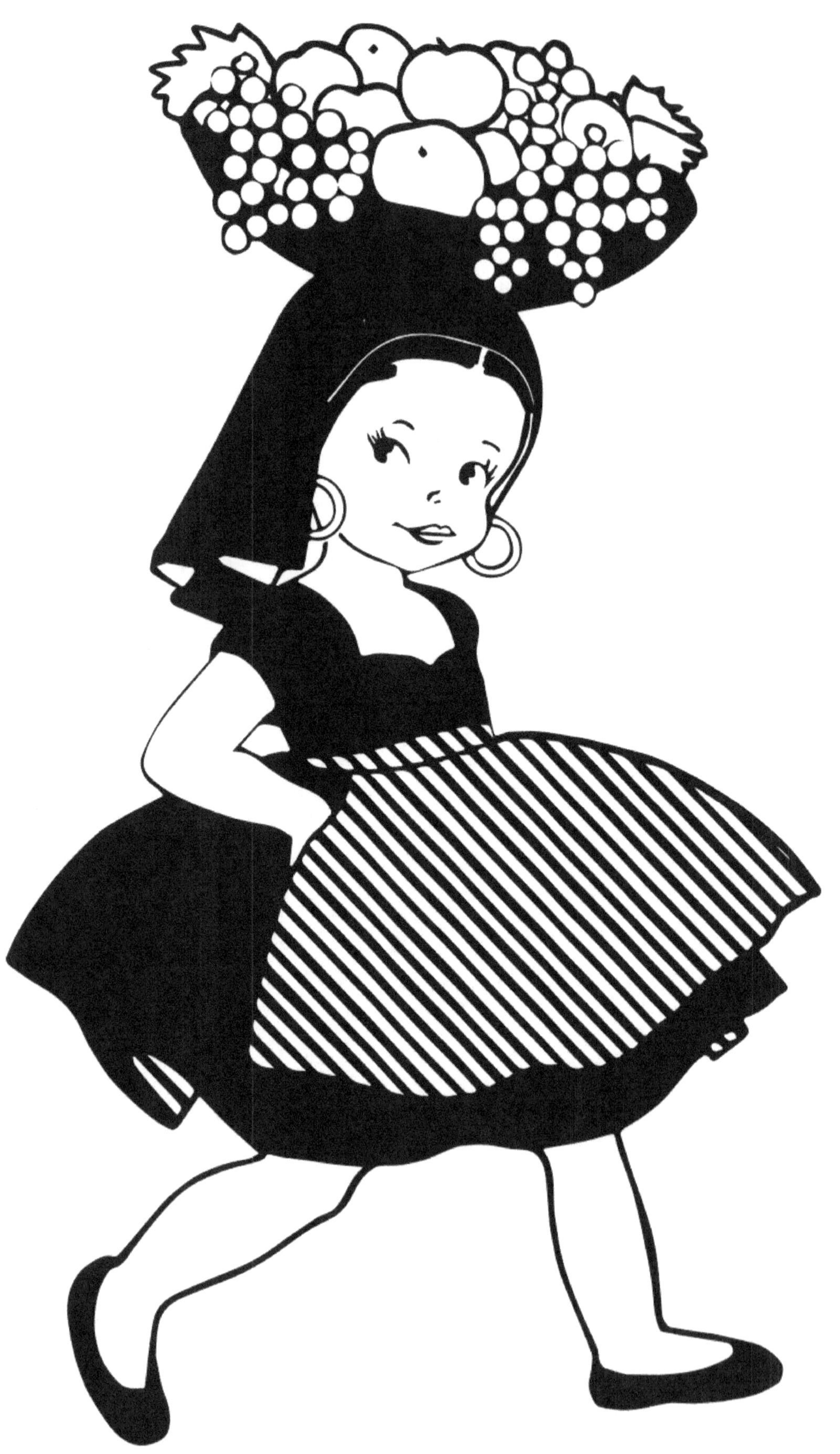

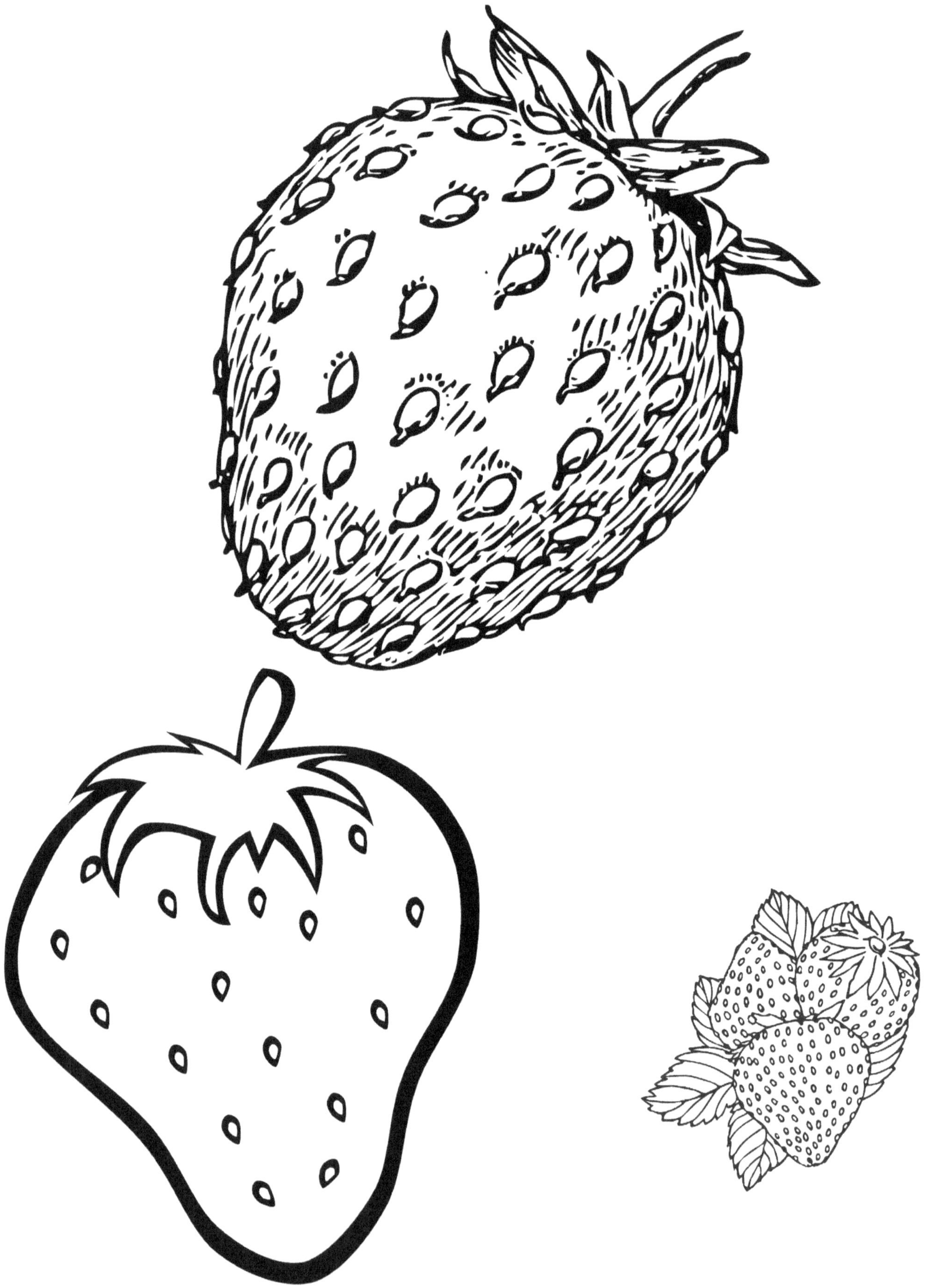

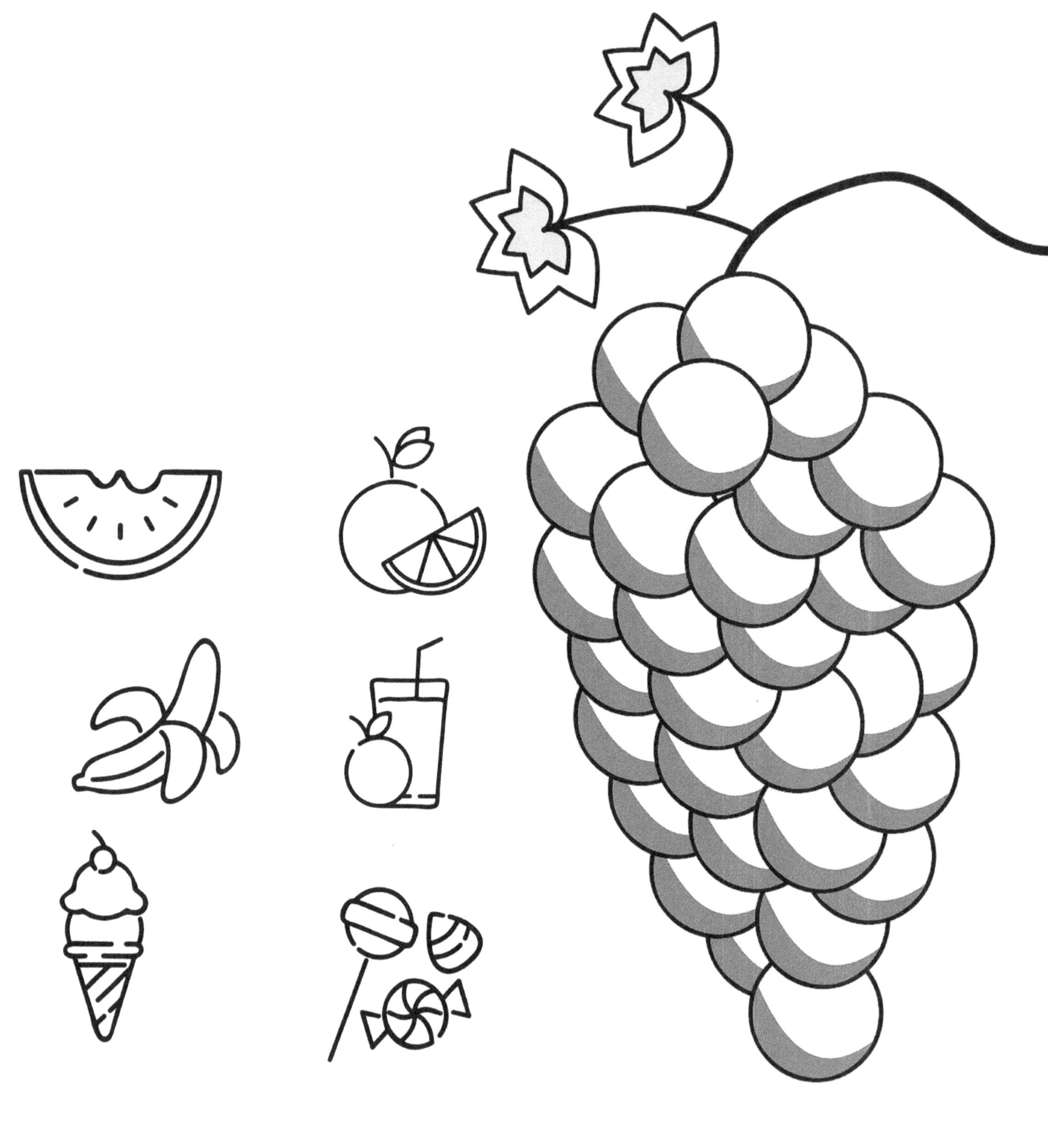

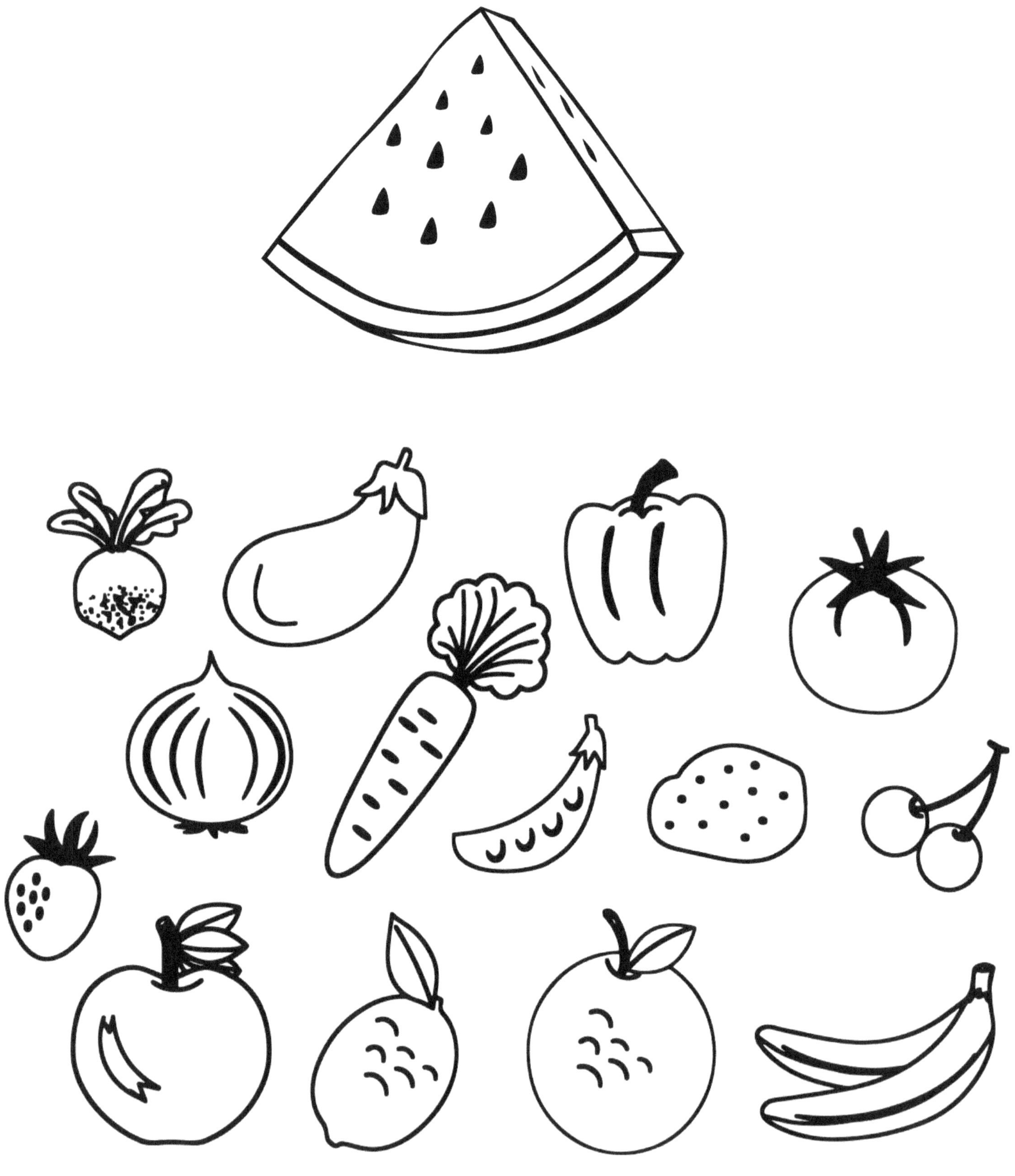

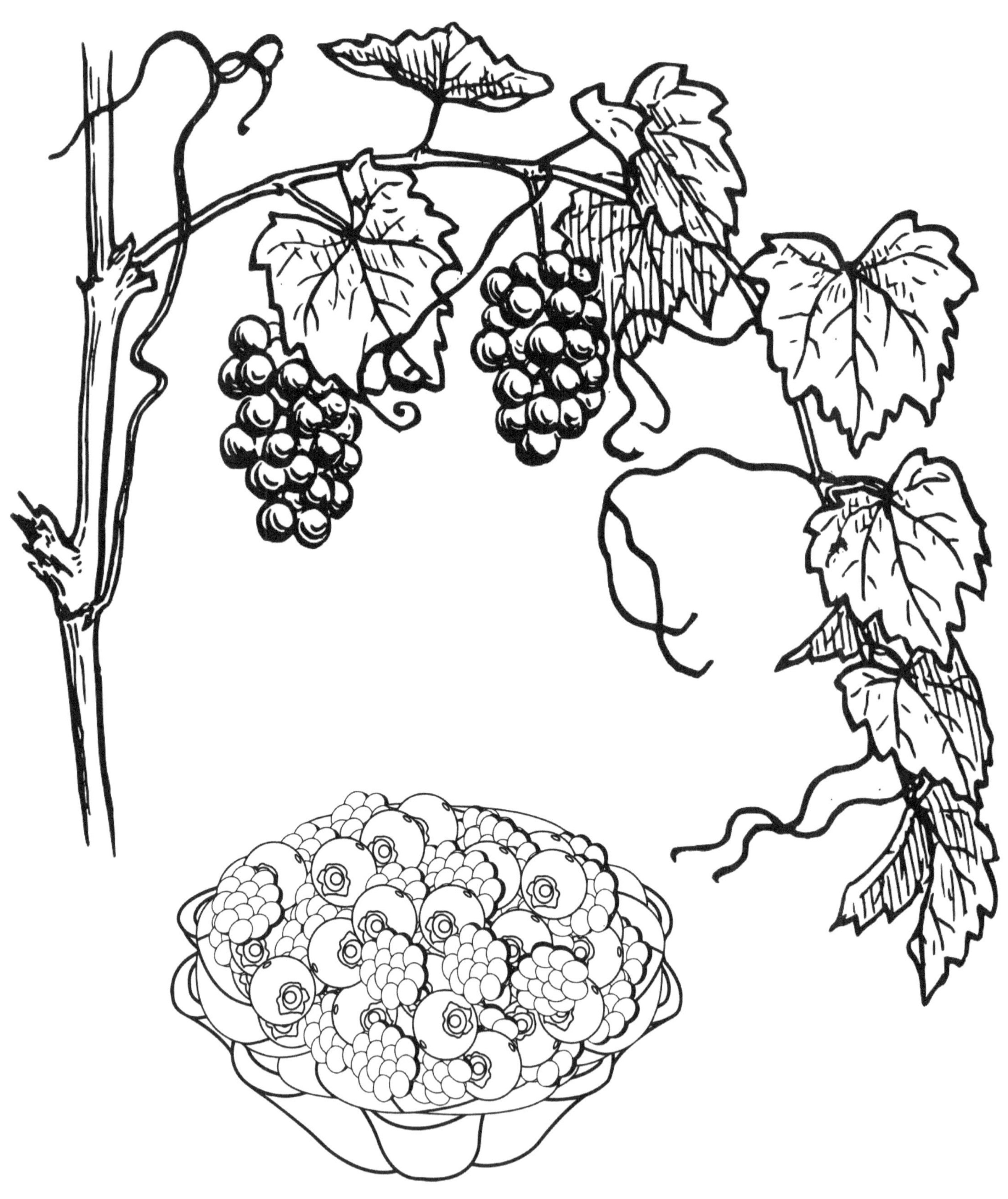

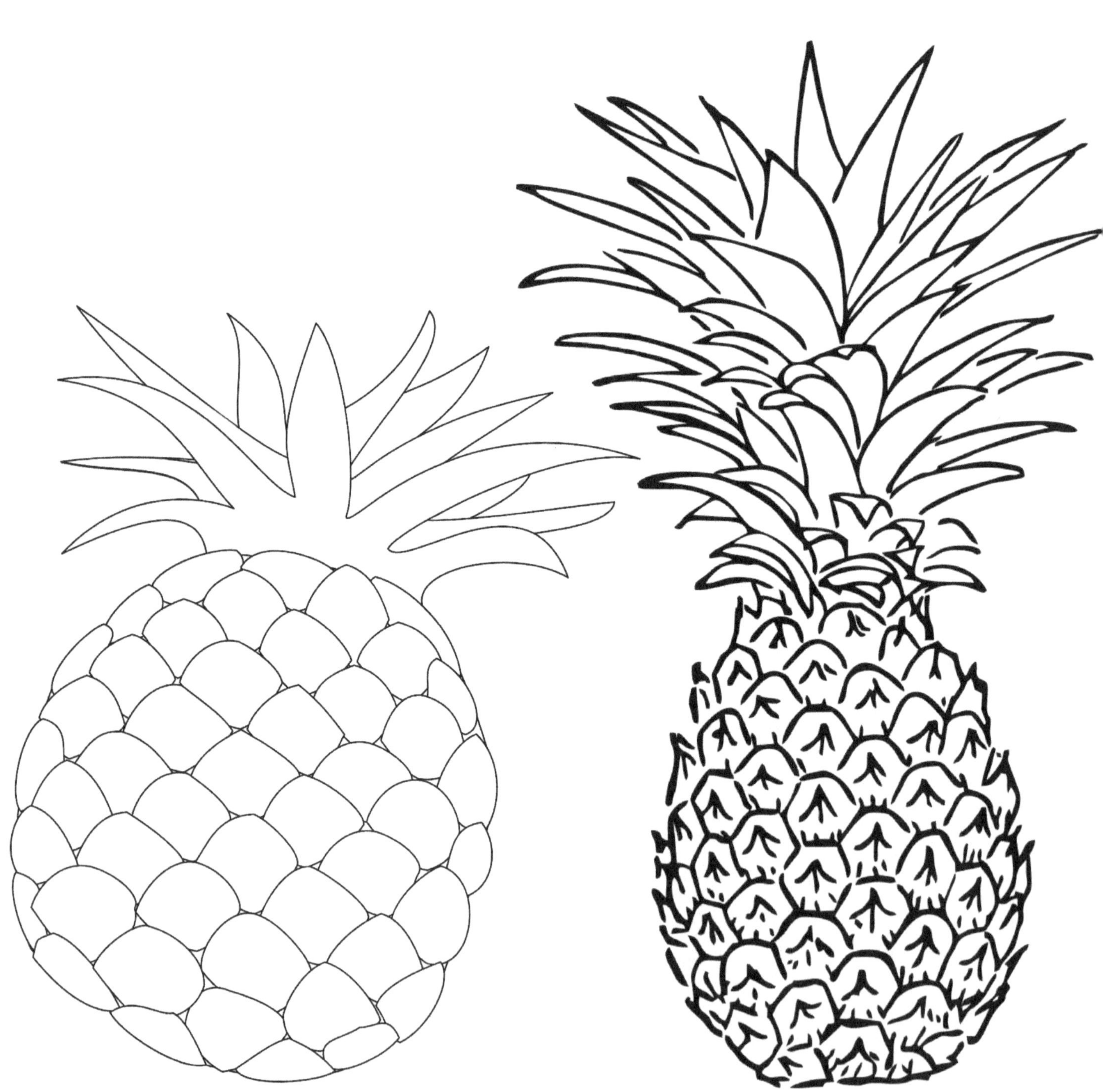

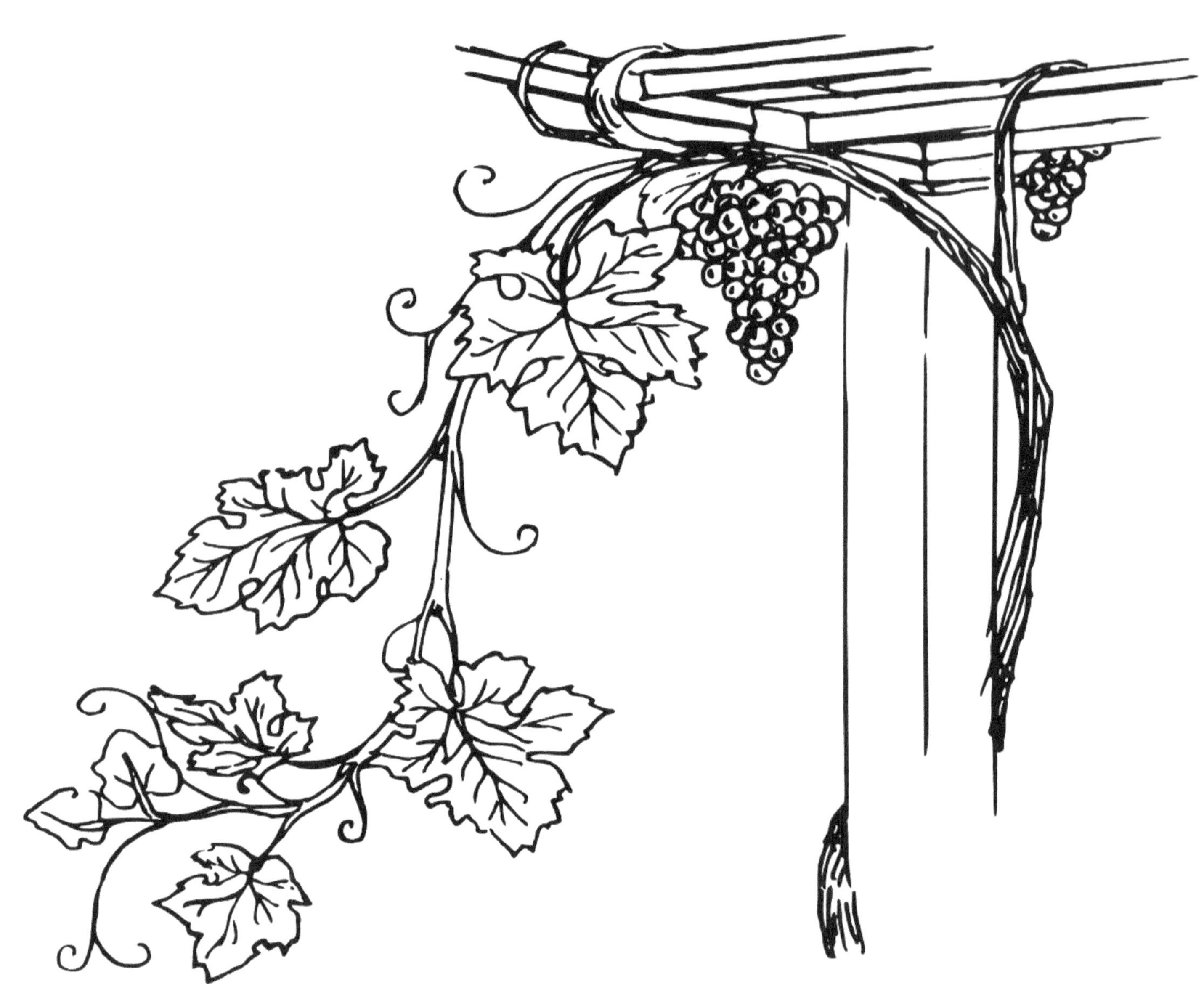

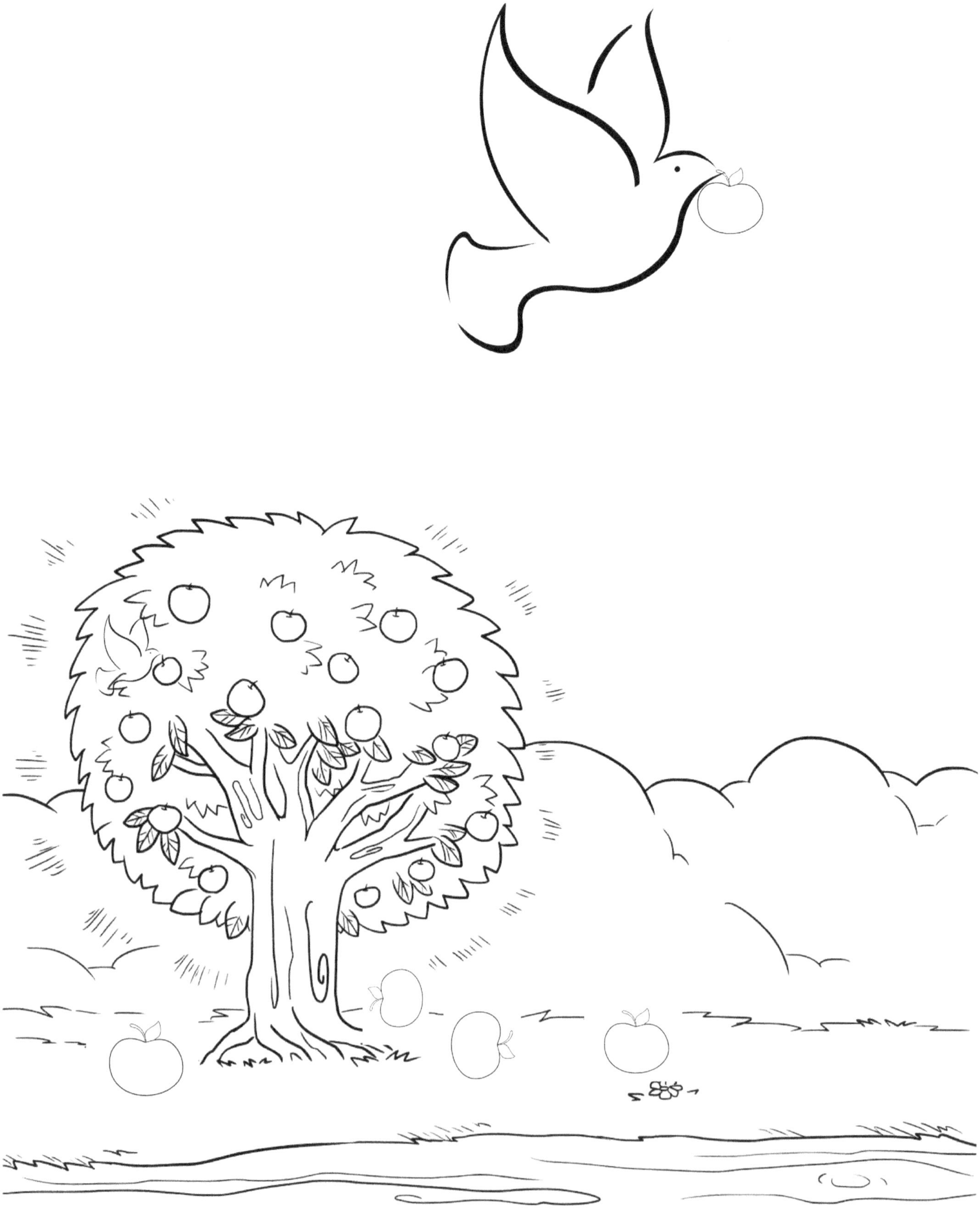

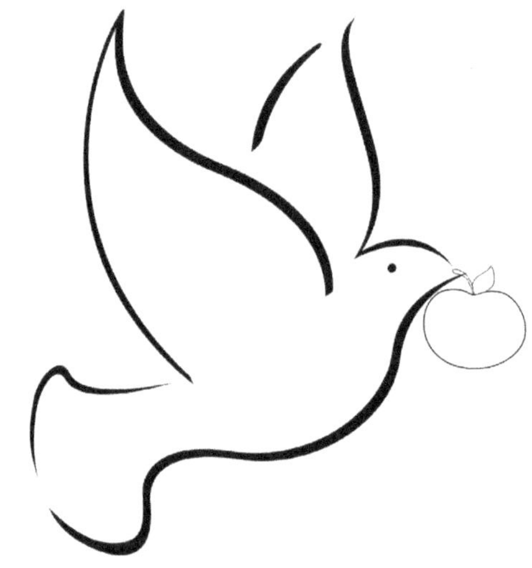

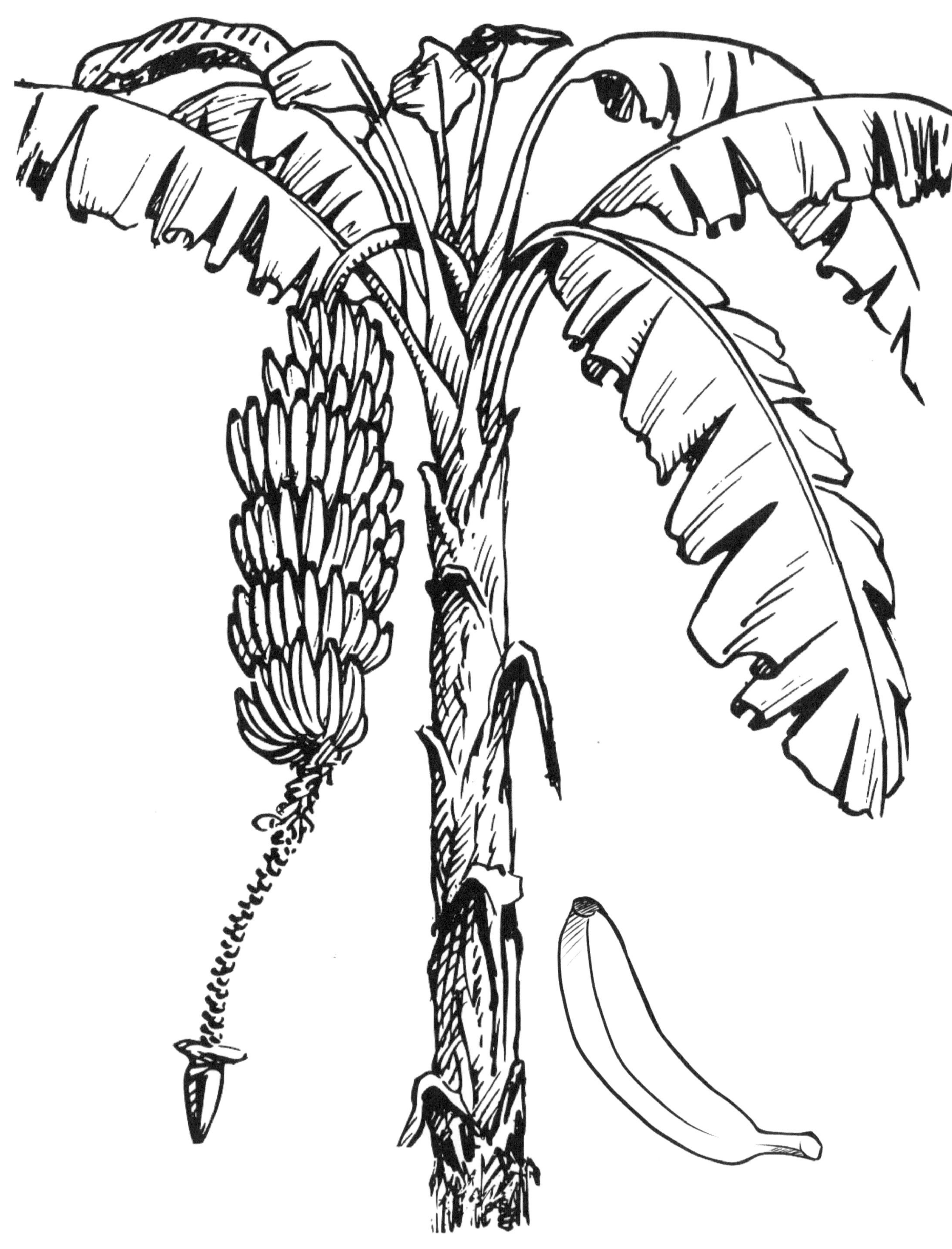

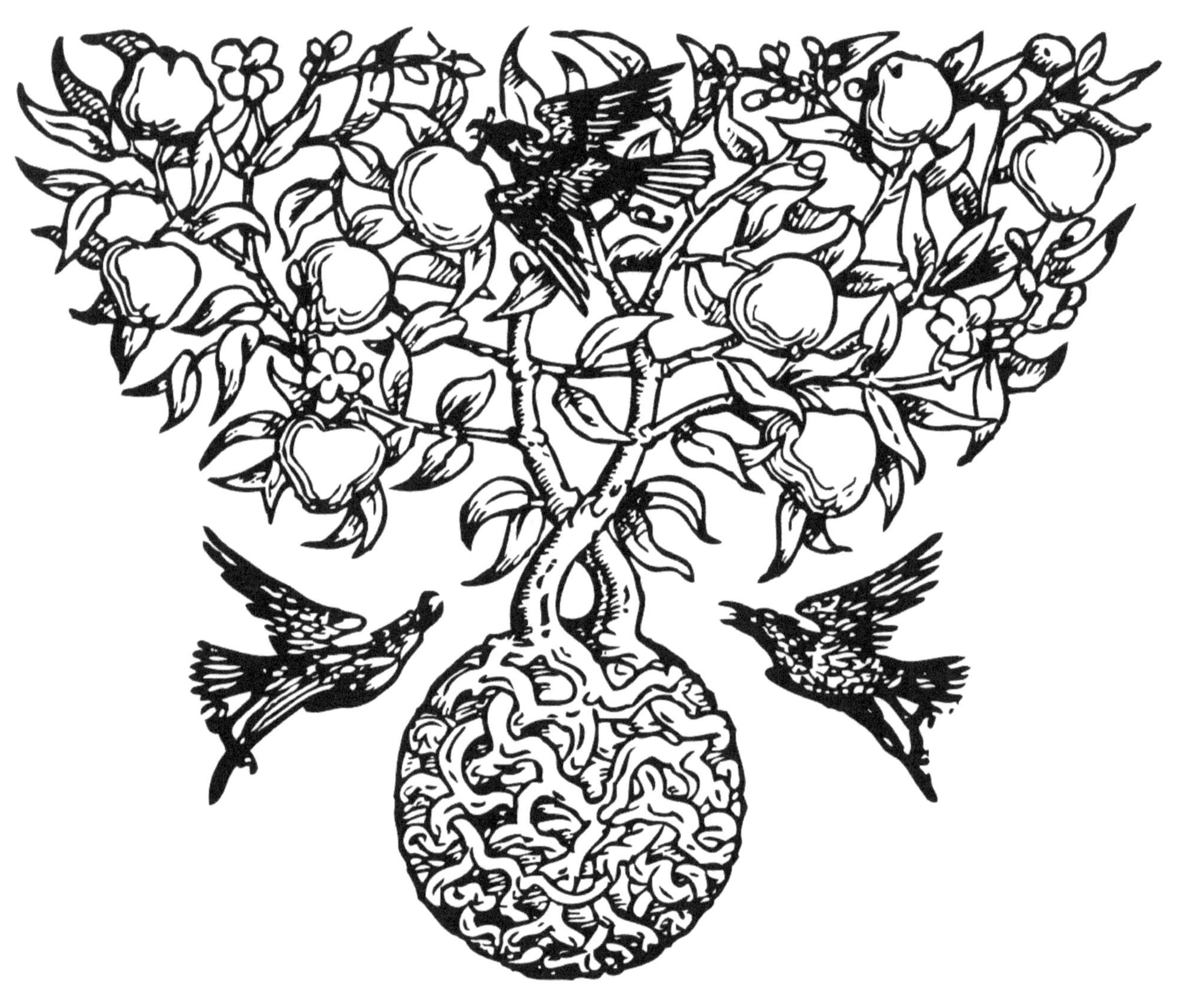

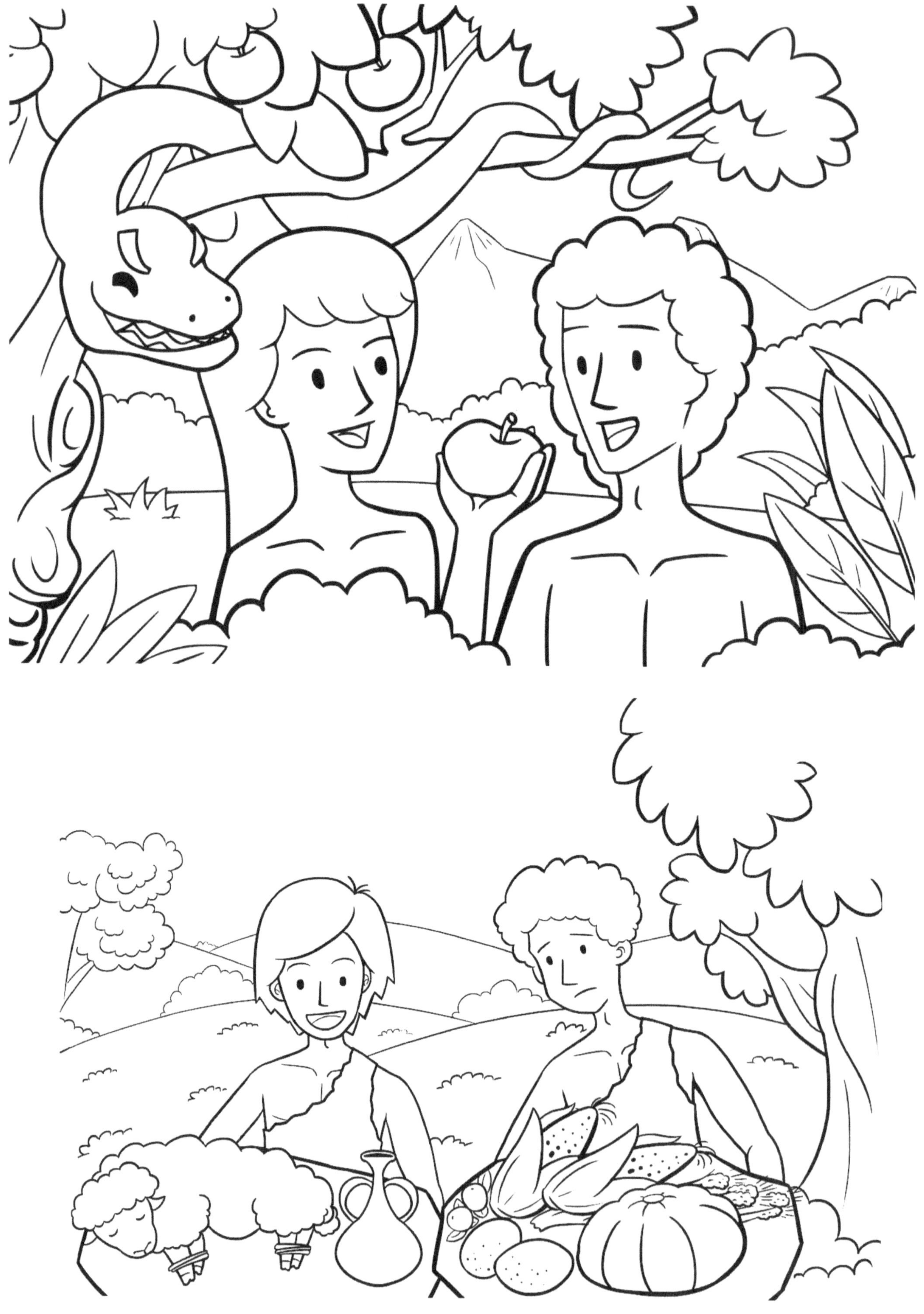

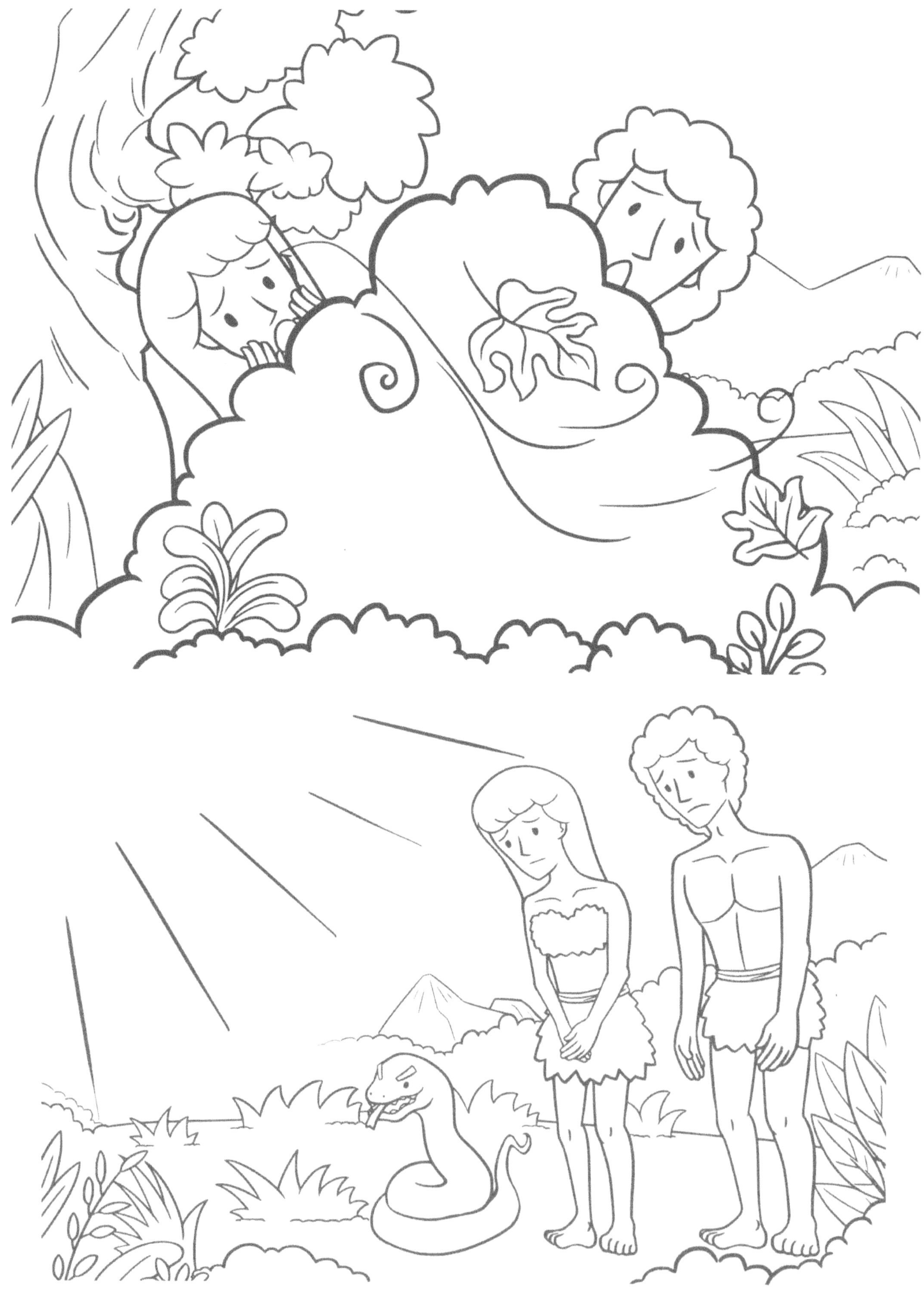

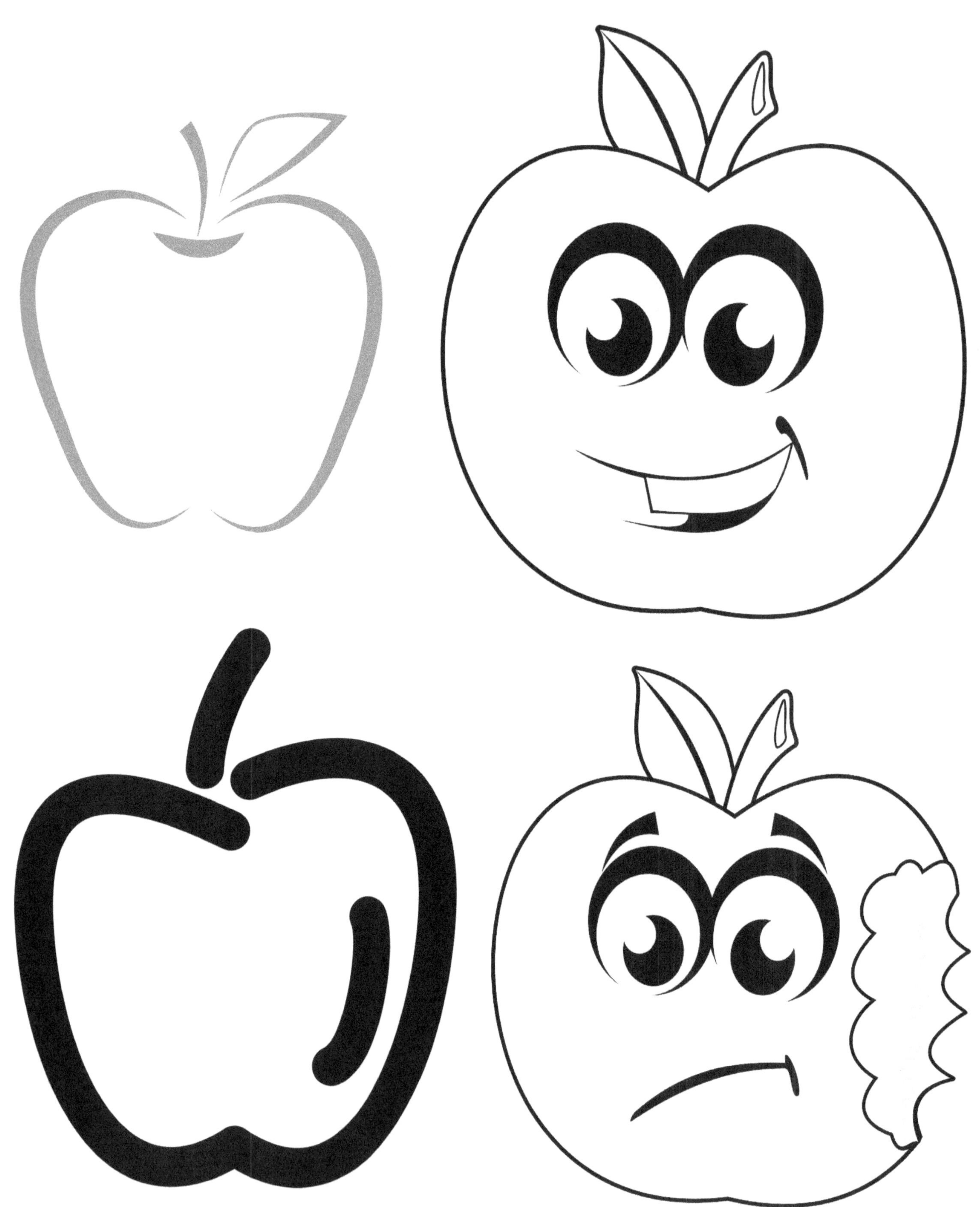

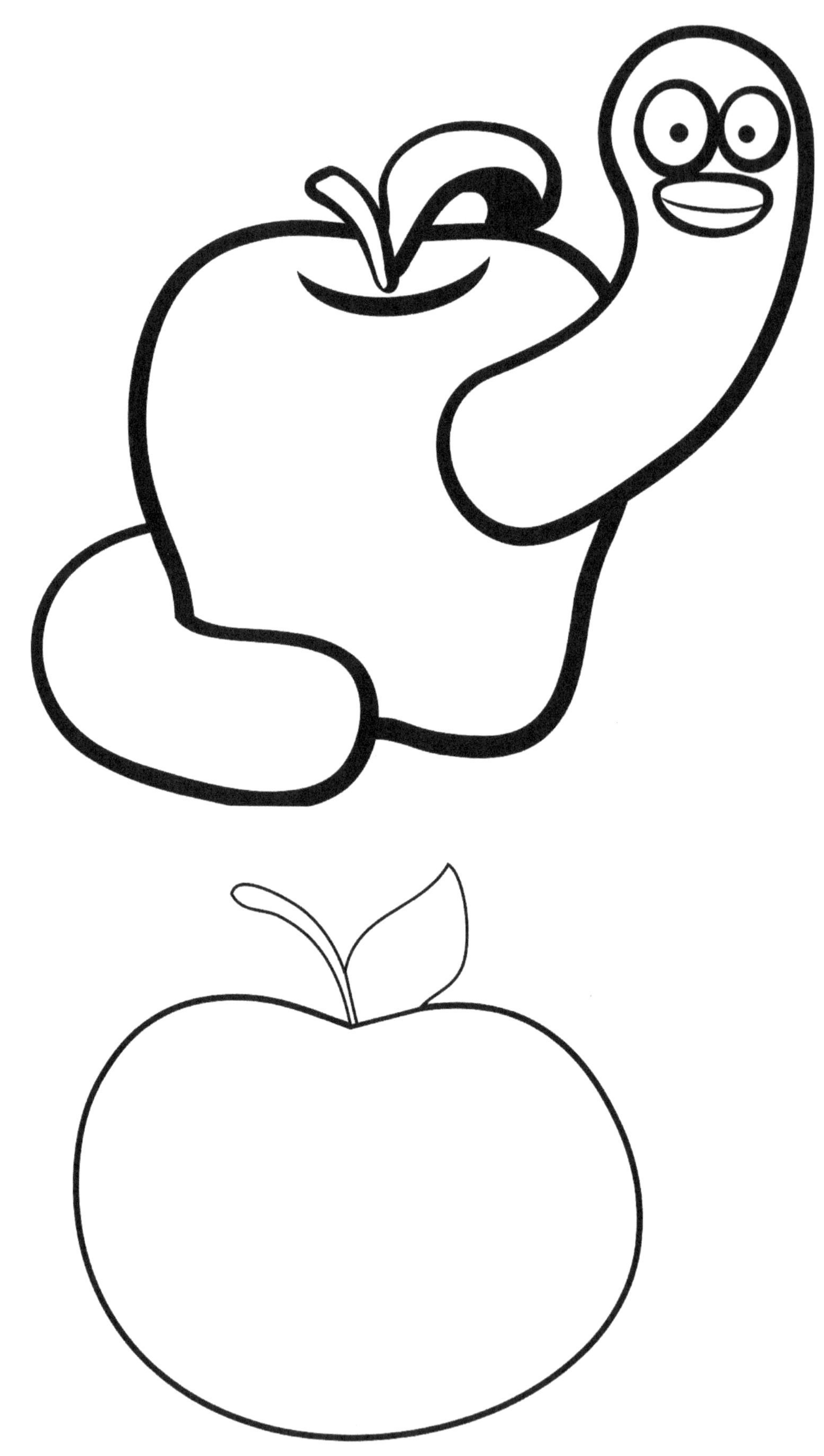

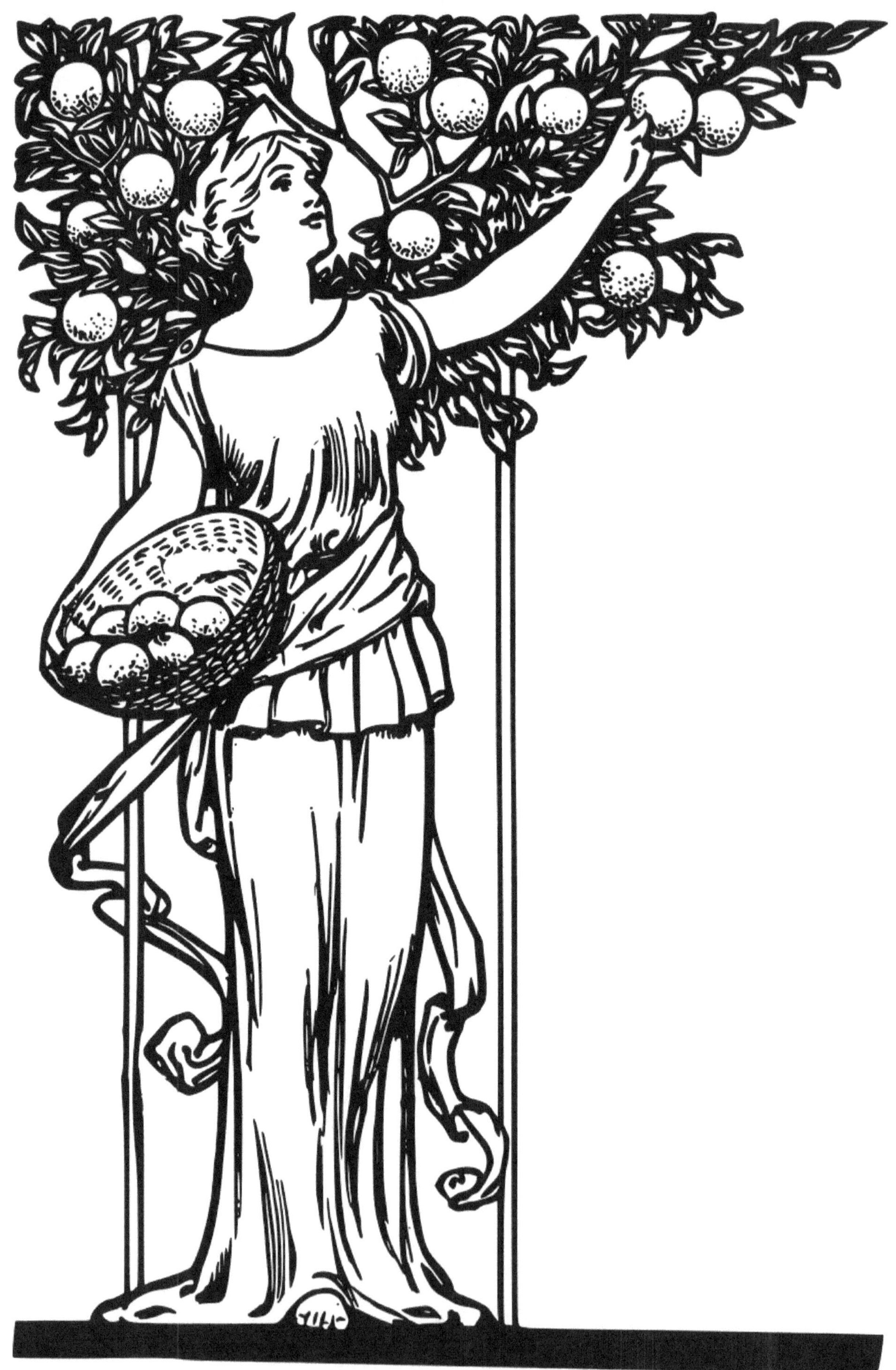

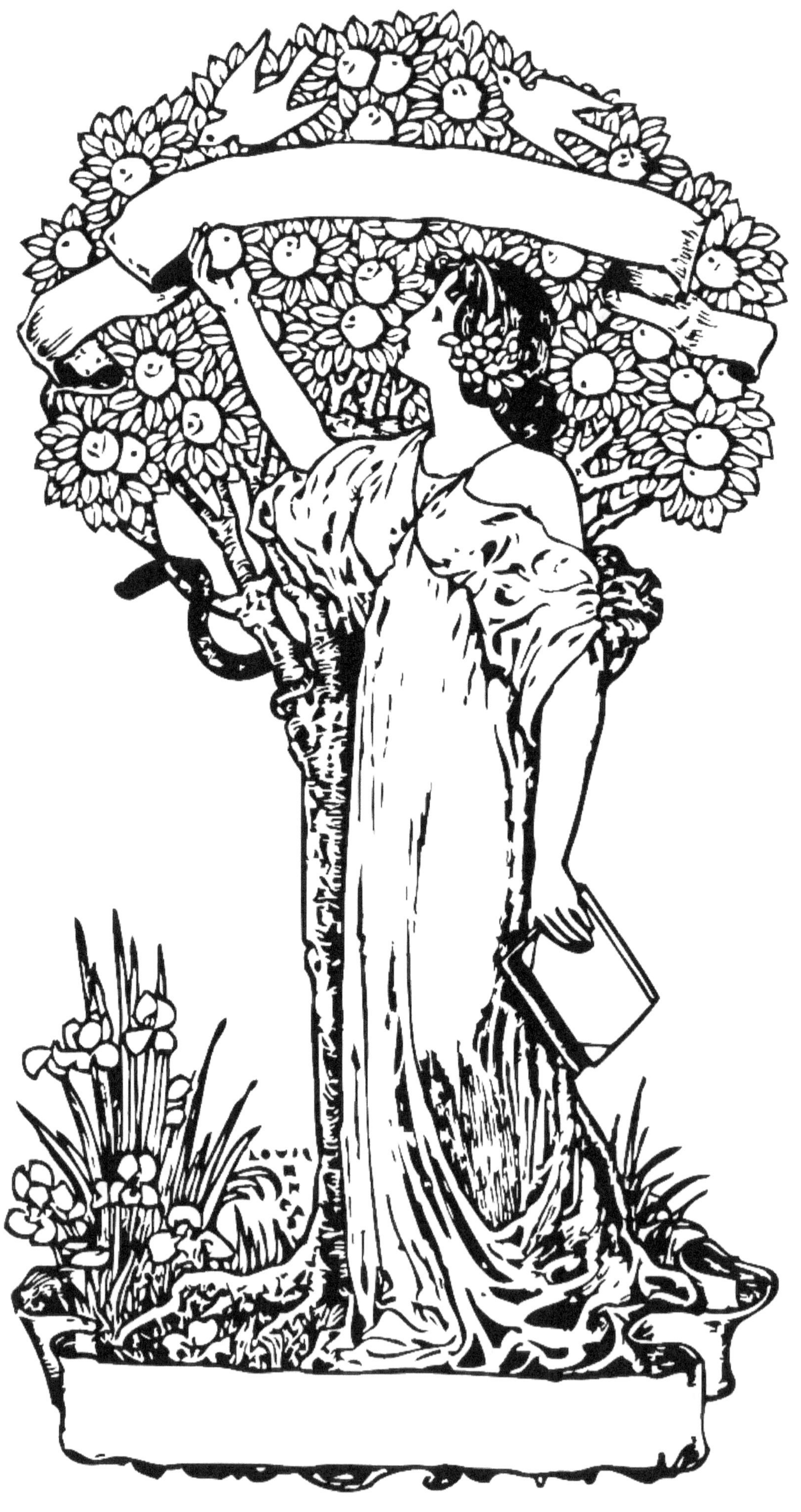

www.ingramcontent.com/pod-product-compliance
Lightning Source LLC
Chambersburg PA
CBHW081025260726
48662CB00026B/3163

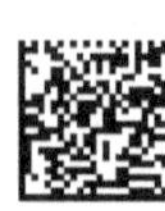